For Gemma-saurus and Vera-saurus

The authors and publishers would like to thank
Dr. Angela Milner, Deputy Keeper of Paleontology at the Natural History Museum, London,
for her help and advice.

First published in Great Britain in 2006 by Frances Lincoln Children's Books, 4 Torriano Mews, Torriano Avenue, London NW5 2RZ
First published in the United States of America by Holiday House, Inc. in 2007
All Rights Reserved
Printed and Bound in China
The illustrations have been done in watercolor and pencil.
www.holidayhouse.com
1 3 5 7 9 10 8 6 4 2

Library of Congress Cataloging-in-Publication Data
Manning, Mick.
Dino-dinners / by Mick Manning ; illustrated by Brita Granström. — 1st ed.
p. cm.
Originally published: London : Frances Lincoln Children's Books, 2006.
ISBN-13: 978-0-8234-2089-6 (hardcover)
ISBN-10: 0-8234-2089-2 (hardcover)
1. Dinosaurs—Food—Juvenile literature. I. Granström, Brita, ill. II. Title.
QE861.5.M3427 2007
567.9—dc22
2006036772

Visit Mick and Brita at www.mickandbrita.com

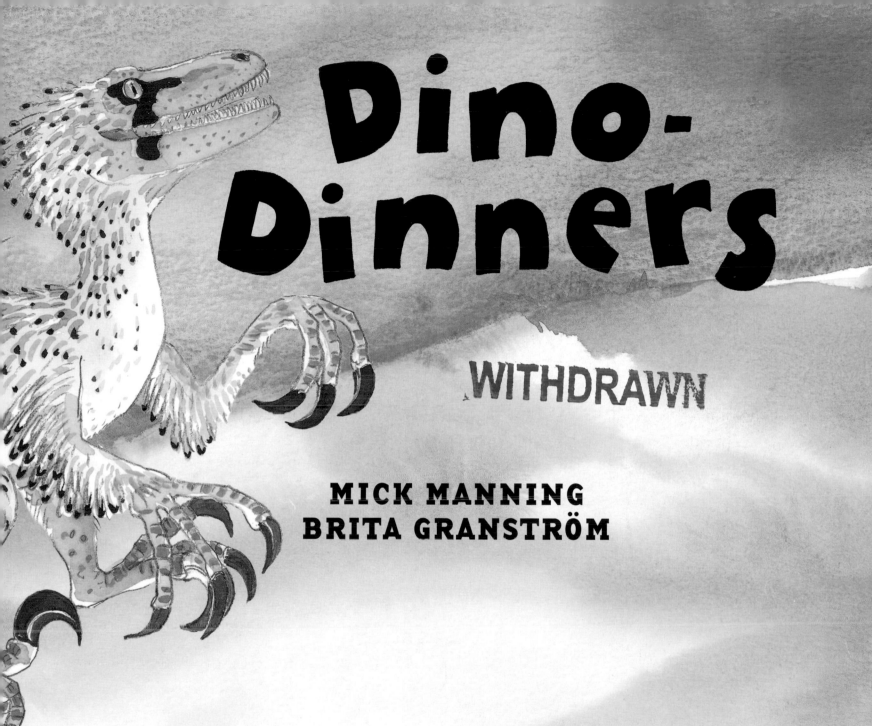

Dino-Dinners

MICK MANNING
BRITA GRANSTRÖM

Holiday House / New York
In association with the
Natural History Museum, London

Oviraptor

I eat pinecones, shellfish, and nuts—
crunchy eggs can be tasty too.
Best of all, a fat, crispy beetle
snatched from the top
of dinosaur poop.

Oviraptor

*(OH-vee-**RAP**-tor)*

* Lived 85–75 million years ago
* Nose to tail: 6 feet (1.8 m)
* Omnivore

Oviraptor stood on two legs and was a fast emu-sized dinosaur.

Nobody is sure what *Oviraptor* ate, but it was probably omnivorous, eating both plants and meat.

Using its strong beak, it could easily have crushed nuts, bones, insects, eggs, and shellfish.

Euoplocephalus

*(YOO-o-plo-**SEF**-ah-lus)*
* Lived 74–71 million years ago
* Nose to tail: up to 23 feet (7 m)
* Herbivore

Euoplocephalus's heavy clubbed tail could break the bones of predators. No predator wants to risk that. A serious injury means "game over."

Euoplocephalus's tail weighed up to 66 pounds (30 kg). Its tailbones were strengthened to swing this heavy weight.

It was armored like a tank and probably crouched low, if attacked, to stop a predator from trying to flip it over onto its back.

Euoplocephalus

Here I come!

Trundling through the woodland plants,

I'm always on the lookout

for danger as I munch.

Armored legs, armored body, armored face,

clubbed tail aswinging—just in case.

Look out!

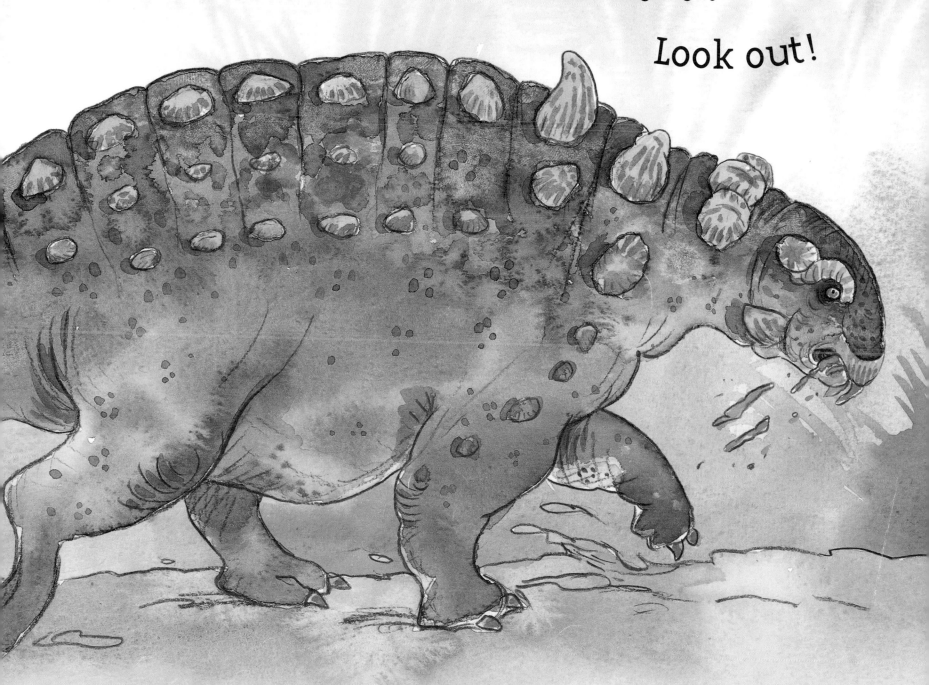

Tyrannosaurus rex

(Tie-RAN-oh-**SORE**-us rex)
* Lived 67–65 million years ago
* Nose to tail: 40 feet (12 m)
* Carnivore

Tyrannosaurus rex's crushing bite and keen sense of smell meant that it could feed on the largest herbivores—alive or dead!

Tyrannosaurus nestlings would have been covered in downy fluff to keep them warm.

Tyrannosaurus rex

I like sick and injured dinos,

or dead dinos that really stink!

I'm a giant with a giant's appetite,

and I love rotten meat—

it doesn't put up a fight!

Triceratops

Triceratops

(Try-**SER**-ah-tops)
* Lived 67–65 million years ago
* Nose to tail: 30 feet (9 m)
* Herbivore

Teeth marks that match *Tyrannosaurus rex* teeth have been found in the fossil bones of *Triceratops*.

Triceratops would have charged like a modern rhino.

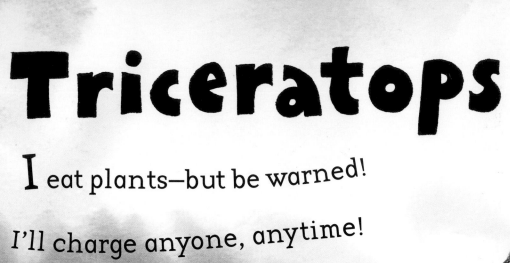

I eat plants—but be warned!

I'll charge anyone, anytime!

My horns have six tons of muscle

and bone behind them.

I am a very dangerous vegetarian.

You'll soon see,

if you ever mess with me!

Edmontosaurus

I am one of a crowd—a herd that trumpets and grunts to each other. My jaws and cheeks help my teeth grind, grate, and crush: turning every delicious mouthful of my veggie dino-dinner into mush.

Edmontosaurus

(Ed-MON-to-SORE-us)
* Lived 76–67 million years ago
* Nose to tail: up to 43 feet (13 m)
* Herbivore

Edmontosaurus was a hadrosaur living in herds in open plains and woodlands.

Its jaws moved in a unique sideways chewing motion, making its teeth act like a cheese grater.

Some hadrosaurs had bony crests. Some called to each other using large "trumpet" chambers in their heads.

Velociraptor

Velociraptor

(Ve-LOS-ee-**RAP**-tor)
* Lived 80–73 million years ago
* Nose to tail: 6 feet (1.8 m)
* Carnivore

Velociraptor was a pack hunter like modern wolves.

Velociraptor had feathers to keep warm. Flapping feathered arms may also have helped it balance.

A *Velociraptor* and a *Protoceratops* were found fossilized together! They died fighting each other and then were covered with blowing sand.

Huge toe claws helped *Velociraptor* climb up onto the backs of large prey.

Big or small, there's no escape
once my gang give chase.
We sprint . . . and leap,

climbing leathery mountains of dino flesh
with the huge claws on our feet.

Then comes our favorite part—

EAT! EAT! EAT!

Coelophysis

(SEEL-oh-FIE-sis)
* Lived 225–220 million years ago
* Nose to tail: 10 feet (3 m)
* Carnivore

Coelophysis lived early in the age of dinosaurs.

Fossilized *Coelophysis* have been found with chewed-up young in their stomachs.

They may well have been under stress from starvation and drought, but this still makes them dino-cannibals.

Coelophysis

We prowl the landscape, hunting for prey.
When times get hard we'll eat
our own kind if they get in our way.

Any bite-sized version of ourselves will do—
a meaty niece, a crunchy nephew. . . .

Iguanodon

Pond plants are a tasty dino-dinner for us.
We browse slowly and quietly,
munching as we move.
Then comes the noisy part—

the more we eat,
the more we fart!

Iguanodon

(I-GWAN-o-don)
* Lived 130–115 million years ago
* Nose to tail: up to 33 feet (10 m)
* Herbivore

Iguanodon used
the "pinkie finger" on each
hand to grip and pull
leafy stems to its mouth.

All that plant food
made *Iguanodon*'s
large stomach fizz up
like a bottle of soda,
producing a lot of gas!

Iguanodon's huge thumb
spike was its only defense
against predators like
Baryonyx.

Baryonyx

Fresh fish are my favorite.

I swipe them with my hooked claws

and swallow them one at a time:

head, fins, and scales—

all coated in slippery slime!

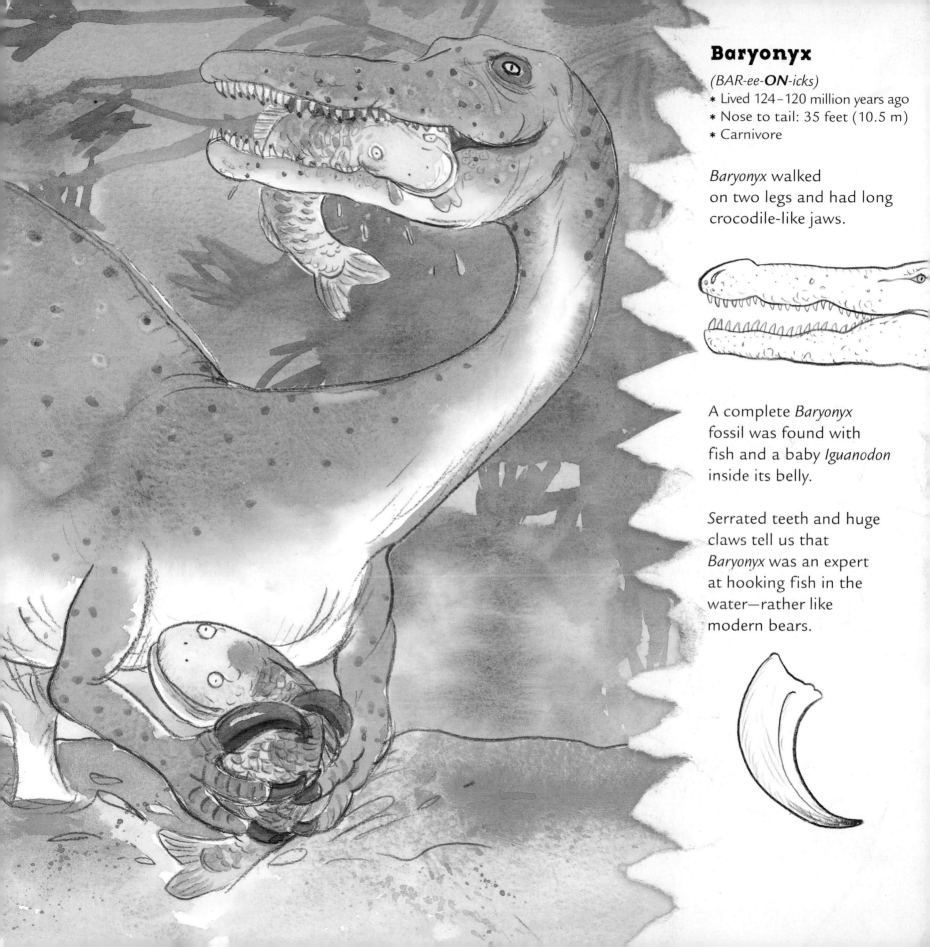

Baryonyx

(BAR-ee-**ON**-icks)

* Lived 124–120 million years ago
* Nose to tail: 35 feet (10.5 m)
* Carnivore

Baryonyx walked on two legs and had long crocodile-like jaws.

A complete *Baryonyx* fossil was found with fish and a baby *Iguanodon* inside its belly.

Serrated teeth and huge claws tell us that *Baryonyx* was an expert at hooking fish in the water—rather like modern bears.

Brachiosaurus

(BRAK-ee-oh-SORE-us)

* Lived 155 – 140 million years ago
* Nose to tail: up to 82 feet (25 m)
* Herbivore

Brachiosaurus and some other plant eaters swallowed small pebbles called gastroliths to help digest the plants they ate.

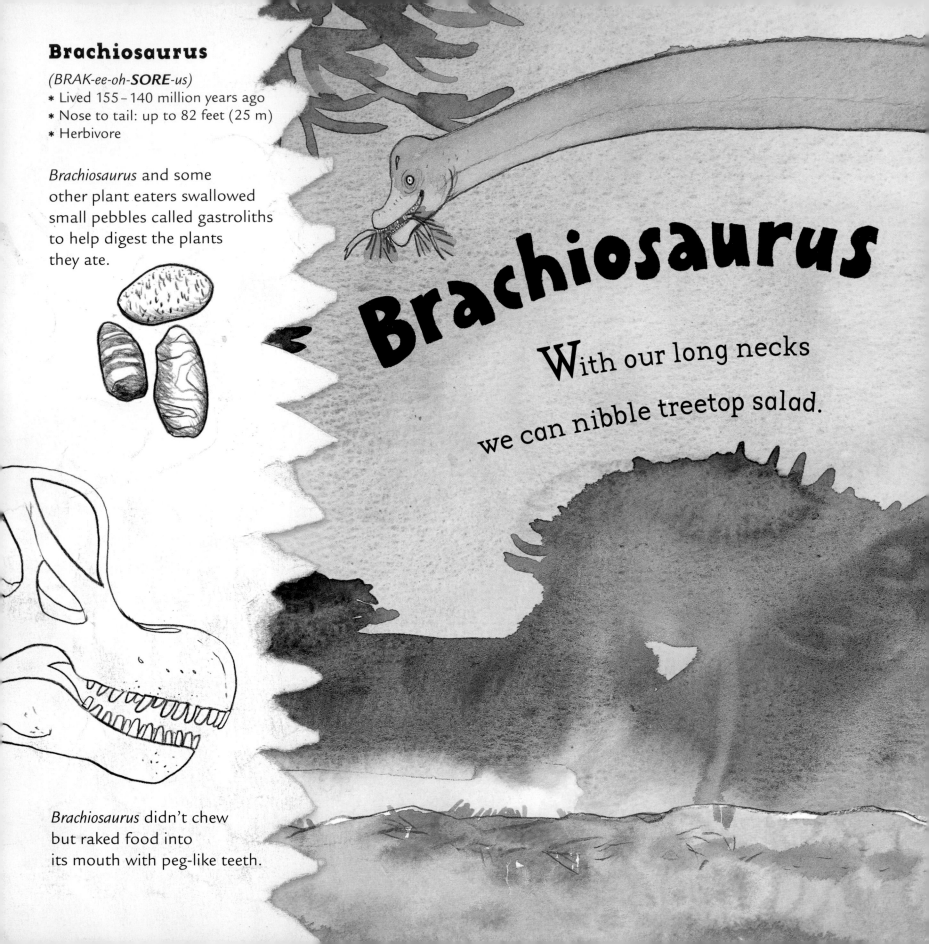

Brachiosaurus

With our long necks we can nibble treetop salad.

Brachiosaurus didn't chew but raked food into its mouth with peg-like teeth.

It tastes green and fresh with
a tangy flavor of pine nuts.

We rake and swallow.

We don't bother to chew.

But treetop salad always makes us . . .

POOP!

The huge amount of plant material *Brachiosaurus* ate meant that it made enormous poops— rather like giant elephant droppings.

Fossil droppings are called coprolites, and they tell dinosaur experts a lot about what dinosaurs ate.

Glossary

Cannibal

an animal that eats other animals of its own kind

Carnivore

an animal that eats only meat

Coprolites

fossilized droppings that can tell us a lot about what different dinosaurs had for dinner

Drought

When it doesn't rain for a long time, plants and animals die because they can't find anything to drink or eat.

Fossil

the traces of animals and plants that have been dead and buried for so long that they turn to stone

Gastroliths

Some plant-eating dinosaurs swallowed pebbles to help them break up the tough plant fibers in their stomachs.

mya = million years ago

248 mya   Triassic   205 mya   Jurassic

Hadrosaur
the name given to the family of "duck-billed," plant-eating dinosaurs to which *Edmontosaurus* belonged

Herbivore
an animal that eats only plants

Omnivore
an animal that eats both plants and meat

Predator
an animal that hunts other animals for food

Prey
an animal that is hunted by other animals for food

Scales
small, hard plates that cover fish, reptiles, and other animals

Serrated teeth
teeth with notches or grooves on their edges that make a good cutting surface, like a knife

Starvation
When there isn't enough food to eat, animals are so hungry that they start to die.

144 mya

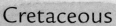

Cretaceous